GROWING GREAT MINDS

The Power, the Necessity, and the Importance of Effective Daycare

Dr. Elaine S. McGhee

Diligence Publishing Company
Bloomfield, New Jersey

GROWING GREAT MINDS

To contact the author email:

eeartdr@aol.com

GROWING GREAT MINDS

ISBN: 978-1-7374840-8-0

Printed in the United States

TABLE OF CONTENTS

DEDICATION

I dedicate my book to my children who have been nothing but supportive. To my son and daughter, Darren and Elissa, it is my hope that life continues to bring the both of you, peace, love, knowledge, and understanding. For these things assist in giving life great value and growth.

To my granddaughter, Shaniah, it is my desire that you will be the perpetual joy, love, and beautiful sunshine of life that will not only afford you great things in life, but also assist others in enjoying life.

ACKNOWLEDGEMENTS

Rev. Dr. Jerome Gourdine

I am thankful and appreciative for your assistance.

Aurelia Grant

I extend my gratitude for your love and support.

Alice Waters

I am grateful for your encouragement.

Tina Watson

I acknowledge your true friendship and trust.

Willie Workman Jr.

I am blessed by your prayers to have faith and never give up.

ENDORSEMENT

To "My Sista 4 Life," Dr. Elaine S. McGhee, the Lord has put in your belly the fire of excellence that exclusively emanates from God and Him alone. You have been a gift to the field of education and childcare for many years, and your ministry of service is unapproachable. This book, which is a labor of love, makes and will make a positive **impact** on those who are blessed to read and study it. You are that beacon of light that all prospective daycare entrepreneurs will be guided by. God speed on "Mysista 4 Life."

Your Bruh 4 Life, Rev. Dr. Jerome Gourdine

FOREWORD

When I was given the opportunity to read the information that Dr. Elaine McGhee gives in this book, I was extremely impressed. Her extensive knowledge of the childcare center industry is very in-depth. My wife, Venessa, has been working as a caregiver in childcare for a long time, which assisted me in relating to this book. I will encourage anyone that may be considering opening and starting a childcare center to utilize the information Dr. McGhee is sharing. Thank you, Dr. McGhee, for sharing your book with me. God Bless you.

Rev. Pastor Alfred A. Dingle Sr.

ABOUT THE BOOK

I am writing this book for the purpose of vehemently and intellectually highlighting the instructions and motivations for those interested in starting their own childcare center. It also offers a view of the concerns of parents and/or guardians of children who are and may be preparing to attend a childcare center. This book will equip those contemplating going into the childcare business. I have attempted to give the necessary information required to help potential center owners and operators. Being able to share this knowledge is a great blessing for me.

Dr. Elaine S. McGhee

"Give me just one generation of youth, and I'll transform the whole world."
"Give me four years to teach the children and the seed I have sown will never be uprooted."
By Vladimir Lenin

INTRODUCTION

I open this book by expressing the passion that I have for the education of children. Because, for society to continue to grow, education must be in the equation. History must be taught to children for them to know the successes and failures of humanity. Mathematics must be taught for the purpose of functioning in business, accounting, architecture, measurements, and any other job that involves the use of numbers. Reading is necessary for obtaining and sharing information, etc. So, for society to continue, education must also continue.

The reason for this book is to motivate people, who have a desire to educate children, to consider working in an area of child education that is not only important, but also extremely rewarding, emotionally and financially, if done properly. That business is childcare. Hopefully after reading this book, the readers will not only be equipped with the necessary information to start and operate a high-quality child daycare center, but also be equipped with the motivation and passion to do so. If you have ever considered operating your own daycare facility and have a dream and desire to do so, I believe that this book can be informational as well as inspirational in bringing your dream from the dream stage to the reality stage.

CHAPTER 1

The Need for High-Quality Childcare

For the past 10 years or more, I have had a hardy and deep concern about the direction of our young children in the urban areas. This is the area in which I was born and raised. Through my studies in college and having worked in the field of education as a teacher, guidance counselor, and administrator, I have come to realize that it is possible for me to do something about my concern through providing information on how to start and operate a well-designed and meaningful, focused, highly qualified and nurturing childcare center.

Our former President Barak Obama, in his State of the Union address said, *"It's time we stop treating childcare as a side issue or a woman's issue and treat it like the national economic priority that it is for all of us to have a good start."*

In this new era, education strives particularly hard in urban schools that house children of poorer areas in disproportionately large numbers. He also stated that, "We're in a new era of responsibility, and childcare should be a part of that era."

There are studies that notify us that children in poorer financial conditions, that are under the age of 4, are at greater risk of decreased cognizant development. Due to the financial challenges that exist in poorer communities, children, that are in these conditions, run the risk of facing poor health and nutrition, insufficient learning opportunities and more. Low achieving tots are at risk of dropping out of school. Having the opportunity to attend a "high quality" childcare center presents an opportunity for them to achieve a higher I.Q. and better growth.

I agree and am an advocate for a loving, safe, stable, age-appropriate, stimulating environment such as a childcare center. Today, America must compete with all other nations in a global economy. If we do not prepare our youth to take on the challenge, we run the risk of losing our competitive edge and perhaps our democratic children. Early development, for them, is vital to

18

later achievements in life. I like to consider this from an "Alphabetical" perspective because our children are:

Amazing
Brave
Courageous
Dynamic
Energetic
Fun
Grateful
Honest
Intelligent
Joyful
Kind
Loving
Magnificent
Nice
Obedient
Positive
Qualified
Respectful
Strong
Trusting
Understanding
Vibrant
Worthy

Xenial

Youthful

Zestful

In this great and growing age of technology, the importance of education, in my opinion, cannot be overly stressed. The possession of a wealthy passion for the increase in knowledge is not only profitable for the individual, but also for society and the world at large. Those who understand the necessity of being educated are active in the promotions of education as well as its hindrances.

There is power in knowledge. Getting an education is especially important. Knowledge can be helpful or harmful depending upon how it is used, to whom it is given, or if the information presented is flawed and/or incorrect. Information can be used to liberate and elevate the minds and aspirations of a person who has goals, dreams, and desires. But inaccurate, flawed, or untruthful information can be used to imprison, degrade, and manipulate. This can cause a lack of productivity in doing that which is right. Therefore, receiving a proper education is vital for the intellectual growth of a person and society.

Education is vital, and the accuracy of the knowledge obtained is needed if there is any chance for it to be used properly and profitably. So, getting a good education is particularly important.

For this reason, how and to whom it is rendered is also important. Everyone should be allowed to receive an education. But history informs us of the grave efforts made to keep the opportunity to be educated out of the grasp of many. Although humanity should have evolved by now, there is a continued dialog many are involved in about education. The discussions in which people are engaged concerning the educational system is increasing day by day, week by week, month by month, year by year, decade by decade and even century by century.

The dialogue involves a multiplicity of topics, methods, finances, and participants. Some of the politicians, business owners and investors, in the city in which I currently reside, appear to be "shifting away" from the priority of public service programs. It appears that the focus is on the development of projects that produce jobs and create job opportunities for residents, for the financial stability of the city. While some at the

21

table intend to include public service programs that also involve free education for residents, some people are presenting proposals to the contrary. But regardless of the outcome of these political debates, discussions or agreements, there will continue to be the need for education. I stressed the importance of education because it is directly connected to the future work force.

This is a great place to speak about the need and the importance of high-quality childcare. For it is in the early years of life that children's minds are like sponges and learn quickly.

The statements that I shared earlier, that were given by the 44th President, Barak Obama, I believe is worth repeating.

"It's time we stop treating childcare as a side issue or a woman's issue and treat it like the national economic priority that it is for all of us to have a good start." President Barak Obama.

The early stages of life are great places to start preparing children with the basic skills that they will need later in life. Giving children a head start will better equip them for future and further learning.

Our communities need high-`quality childcare and people who possess a great desire and dream to be in the business. Who is up for the challenge?

CHAPTER 2

More Than Just Babysitting Understanding the True Purpose of Childcare

There are specific businesses that remain to be in constant demand. Childcare is one of those businesses that society will continue to be in need of as long as people want to have families. Although I desire to motivate and stress the need for childcare facilities to be established, it is extremely important that I stress this fact. Anyone who plans on working in this field of childcare must have a strong desire and passion to care for children. Anyone that intends on starting, owning, and operating a daycare center must be aware that it is more than being a babysitter.

This business requires love for children, patience, and a mind for business. There are many rules and regulations involved in operating any business and child daycare is no different. Babysitting can already be somewhat of a challenge, especially, if some unexpected circumstances arise. But when you have to make sure that the proper paperwork is in order, it can be stressful. There are many guidelines required by the city, state and federal government that must be adhered to for your center. That is why having the right information and the right staff is vitally important.

Just merely having a good heart is not enough to run an effective daycare center. Just having the money is not enough to be successful in the childcare field. Not only does it take planning, but it also takes a great understanding of what impact your center can have on growing minds.

When you understand that your center can be a nurturing center to help children get prepared for the next stages in their lives, your drive for being successful means that your attendees will be better prepared for the future. Other information will be given in the next chapters of this book, but it is absolutely necessary that it is relayed that the motives for starting a center are the right motives. It's not about just making money. In other words, you must maintain the

26

true purpose of your vision. You must continue to remember why you are going or have gone into the child daycare business in the first place. Your drive must overshadow your challenges. Your passion and love for the well-being of children must override the problems. You must remember your purpose. It is about growing great minds.

CHAPTER 3

Starting Your Childcare Facility and Mission

High-quality childcare is an essential component of life in our society, and it will assist with our children's readiness to be successful in school as they grow and move up to other grades and levels of education.

These are the things you would need to know and do to prepare for your childcare center. One of the first things that needs to be done is making a Financial Plan. You need to establish a budget. You need to know what you can afford and how much you may possibly need to operate. Without that, you are headed for trouble before you begin. All the other information rendered here will be unbeneficial if you are not aware of how much money is needed to start and open your facility.

Once that is organized then other steps can be made.

• Prepare a Financial Plan

• Secure financing.

> Private Sources
> Commercial Banks
> Government Agencies
> Grant Programs

• Secure adequate quality insurance.

• Employ a certified director with a strong sense of responsibility, strong communication skills, strong leadership and management abilities.

• Find a great location with enough square feet to accommodate infants, toddlers, and preschool children for classrooms and special offerings.

• What's in a name? Find the perfect name for the daycare center. The name is important, unique and/or personal, therefore, it should be distinguishable. Helpful tips:

> 3 words or less
> Easy pronunciation
> Easy spelling
> Cute

➢ Catchy

➢ Original

• Request an informal inspection.

• Get state approved license needed to operate a functional facility for a childcare center.

• Equip the classrooms with appropriate furniture.

• Position specific curriculum materials in the classroom.

• Bring staff on board. A dedicated, qualified staff will meet the needs of the children through providing an exclusive developmental curriculum tailored specifically for exploring, experimenting, observing, talking, absorbing, and relating. The staff will also focus on assisting the children develop physically, mentally, emotionally, and socially by providing a nurturing environment. The staff will also try to nurture the children's ideas and imaginations.

• Parental involvement through a variety of activities as well as an open-door policy will be encouraged.

• School calendar. The annual school calendar is a representation of the school planning for the whole year which should also include when school ends, holidays, half days of school.

• Daily schedule. The routine way of managing the class daily.

• Child-Parent Pledge. Agreement or promise to assist with a commitment to learn.

• Mission Statement. Explanation of why the child center exists. The first day of the center's opening can be both very exciting and challenging. This is the very reason why you need to have a plan. Benjamin Franklin made a statement that said, *"If you fail to plan, you are planning to fail."*

The childcare center presents an opportunity to make a difference in children's lives and assist in shaping their experiences through learning, exploring, growing, and playing. The strategic plan will establish a focus to ensure a positive direction for the childcare center to go forth.

STAFF:
The staff should consist of qualified, caring, and friendly people with positive attitudes.

Responsible, enthusiastic, disciplined, patient, flexible, creative, good communication skills, organized, have a sense of humor, and low child-to-teacher ratio.

CODE of ETHICS:
• Impartiality
• Respectful
• Honesty
• Considerate
• Integrity
• Words Chosen Wisely
• Trustworthiness
• Avoiding Harmful Words
• Loyalty
• Adherence to N.J. State Law

CURRICULUM:
• Stimulating outlines of lessons needed to meet educational goals. i.e., "Creative Curriculum" featuring exploration and discovery as a way of learning to develop the children's confidence.

MEALS:
• Healthy food and drink that include offering a variety of nutritious choices.

PLAYTIME:

• Age-appropriate toys, puzzles, musical toys, blocks, play phones, outdoor toys to ride on, color forms, sensory toys, dolls, Leapfrog, Disney and Fisher Price toys and maneuverable dramatic play items.

SAFETY and CLEANLINESS:

• Floors, walls, and kitchen.
• Toilets and diaper changing stations.
• No trash left standing.
• Heated, well-lit, and ventilated classes.
• Hands washed regularly as well as masks.
• Play equipment washed and in good repair.
• Play area inside and outside secure.

The childcare center's readiness through planning is the pathway to a healthy, safe, and exciting environment. Hosting an open house for the childcare center should be the next order of business. Your open house will provide an opportunity to share with families a picture of your childcare's symbols, themes, and purpose and intent to nurture the young minds that may attend your center. The theme of my center I chose to use was the concept of a garden. The way the gardeners nurture and care for a garden and help plants grow, was the same concept I chose to use for the children entrusted to me at my childcare center. I viewed them as a garden which had stages of care, and it was my job to nurture them so their minds would grow. That is why the name and theme I selected for my center was "KIDDIE GARDEN." I chose that name and theme because I wanted it to be about growing great minds. What can assist you in preparing for your open house is to remember the Five Double-u (5W) method.

Let's begin with the **Who:**
As you are organizing your list of invitations to distribute, remember that you have a specific goal in mind which is to inform people about your center. Because of this goal, who you invite and what you will display about your facility is of the utmost importance. Remember, every family's tots should be considered as potential attendees, and every friend is a potential advertiser for your business. Also, your caregivers and staff are instrumental in the image of your center.

What:

What, is your Open House? A first impression is a lasting one, therefore the positive impression you give parents, will be considered successful if they have fun and are excited at the open house. You will be judged on the showcase you present.

When:

Plan your open house on a day you think most people are available. Be mindful of holidays. If you choose a Friday or Saturday, early afternoon is recommended. Teachers should take an active part in the open house to assist with parents and the children. Your caregivers and staff should come not only to work but to share in the festivities of the open house. The staff must be dressed to impress, prepared to answer questions to help ease parents' fears, and prepared to work as a team to get the year off to a positive start. The teachers will present your center's theme as well as introduce the curriculum. There should be books, games, puzzles, activities, toys, crafts, and activities for the children to help keep them occupied. This will minimize interruptions while the teachers are addressing the parents. Applications for the enrollment of potential children/attendees should be available to be completed. Teachers should also have handbooks for parents, class activities, and copies of the curriculum overview available as handouts.

Where:

The best place to present your center, is at the center. This way your potential clients can have a visual of the facility their child or children will be attending. As I mentioned earlier, a first impression is a lasting one. Therefore, a positive impression will give parents or guardians something to consider when choosing a childcare center. Success is determined by if your attendees have fun and are excited at the open house. You will be judged on the showcase you present. Lastly, some light refreshments and a calm sound of soothing music will help set the atmosphere for the impression you want to leave upon the attendees. The healthy snacks should include fruit, vegetables and dip, and cheeses or crackers. It will ensure that nutrition is important. Serve bottled ice water and perhaps fruit juice, which is a healthier alternative than soda. It is "still a good thing" to send a thank you note. So, a thank you should be sent to everyone that attended and all who participated in the childcare open house.

Why: Why you should strive to have a successful open house is to impress the parents/guardians of children whose children will attend your center and to acquaint everyone with the center's program. Remember, every child, that attends your open house with their family, is to be viewed as a potential attendee. As was mentioned earlier, first impressions are lasting ones. Someone said somewhere, "You will never get another chance to make a first impression." The growth and the success of your childcare center will depend upon what parents think of you, your staff, your facility, and curriculum. The open house gives you an opportunity to showcase your center and what it intends to be about. Also, it not only allows families an opportunity to get familiar with your center, but also with your staff. Lastly, the staff get an opportunity to get familiarized with each other. Centers always function better when coworkers are comfortable working with each other.

Here is a summary of the childcare center's open house using the 5W method.

Who? Prospective families, children, friends, caregivers, and staff.

What? Open House.

When? On a day and time people are available.

Where? Childcare center.

Why? To impress the parents/guardians of the children so that their children will attend your center, and to acquaint everyone with the center's program.

The children are now "ready to learn," "teachers ready to teach," and "parents ready to transition" their child from home to school for an extended period of time.

The dream of the childcare center can be successfully put into action. Through trust, caring, and dependable contact with each child and with the strong support for family bonding, it will be able to meet the needs of the proposed age groups of children.

CHAPTER 4

Reaching the Parents of Tots by Understanding Parental Intent

It is the desire of good parents/guardians to protect their children from any hurt, harm and danger. Good parents/guardians want to prepare their children for the realities of the world. Plus, they want to create steppingstones towards educational success, along with wisdom to help them with happiness and certainty. Many parents and guardians already face the difficulty of leaving their child in the care of someone else. Some have concerns about leaving their child with someone they know, let alone strangers. So, it is important to hold this fact in consideration.

You, your staff, and the center's appearance must present an atmosphere that will ease some of the parents/guardians' fears. The reality of the matter is that these parents/guardians are placing the responsibility of caring for their child in you and your staff's hands. Therefore, it is necessary to understand their expectation, that the care given to their child will be nothing less than the care they would give their child themselves. People already have enough things that concern them. The last thing they want to or need to worry about is if their child/children are being cared for properly. If parents/guardians believe that caregivers will treat the children like they are their own, it minimizes their worries.

I also want to address that there are some parents/guardians who may not know the actuality of unpleasant realities that their child may be experiencing. Their interactions with their child may be greater if it is realized. Life is not easy or perfect. For this reason, many of the issues that parents/guardians endure, tend to affect the children. Some of the issues can involve the following:

• Financial challenges
• Stress when caring for sick children
• Not persistent in teaching or disciplining their child.
• Lack of love, for a child to be truly happy
• Parents too busy to interact with child

• Lack of support

How these issues affect the children will be discussed later in this book. If parents/guardians know the actuality of the unpleasant realities, they can be ready for it. The reading of books to their children, singing songs, playing games with numbers and letters by parents/guardians, can provide the additional nurturing and stimulation that will be beneficial to the child. Being aware of the intent of the parents/guardian will assist you in designing a better curriculum and presentation to them. If they are of the impression that the center's agendas are in line with their own and what they want for their child, they will be more comfortable with their child attending your facility.

CHAPTER 5

What Parents and Guardians Need To Look for In "High-Quality" Childcare

I have many years in the education system. Within those years, I have encountered many children and parents. When I started my childcare center, this thought came to mind, *"WOW!.... Do parents and/or guardians even know what to look for in "high quality childcare? What are they looking for?"*

Through my many years of experience, I have come to understand this. They all are basically looking for the same things for their child. They are looking for comfort, safety, and fun. They also want their child's social, mental, and physical development to be stimulated and motivated. The key to being educationally successful begins with how to accept and follow up on the approach to education. For any parents that maybe using this information as a guide to select a quality childcare center, think positive and move in the right direction in choosing "high-quality" childcare for the 'apple of your eye.'

It is helpful to have some idea of the mindset of parents in understanding what they may be looking for when selecting a childcare center.

In my experience, I have observed that one of the most significant individuals in the life of a young child is their mother. Not that fathers do not play a role in today's time, but I'm speaking from what I have experienced down through the years. The percentage of mothers who qualify and desire to be a part of my city's workforce, with children under the age of five, in work programs, need affordable, high-quality childcare.

The creation and operation of programs and centers will also assist working mothers of a young child or young children by expanding the availability and access to health services, as well as promoting healthy lifestyles by emphasizing a nutritious diet and physical activity. The fathers' involvement in the health and development of their child and or children have increased in the past ten years in many ways. They offer unique

46

perspectives and have positive effects on their child's emotional well-being and provide a feeling of security. Some challenges for fathers in relating to their child when they are young is knowing what they want and what they need. Fathers do different things than the mothers. A father may be a biological, foster, or adoptive father, a stepfather, or a grandfather. He may not have legal custody or be a resident in the home. Fathers have been forgotten contributors. Fathers have a positive effect on learning.

Childcare has become an essential component of life in our society. We must therefore commit to the purpose that learning begins at birth. I believe that the first years of a child's life are by far the most important in helping to lay the foundation for all intellectual growth and development to follow. It takes a big heart to shape little minds. The preparations that can be given to children in the operations of a childcare center will help them to enter school ready to learn. It will also assist mothers of the young children by expanding the availability and access to health services, as well as promote healthy lifestyles by emphasizing a nutritious diet and physical activity. The learning experiences offered at childcare centers are designed to promote a nurturing environment for the children being cared for to grow and develop physically, mentally, and socially. Learning depends on the input children are given. There are pitfalls to avoid.

This is a framework of a "high-quality" childcare center. In your search to select, observe if it consists of the following:

- Childcare License
- Certified Staff • Staff Training in Early Childhood Experience (CDA)
- Certified Director/Supervisor
- Professional and Stable Teaching Workforce
- Effective Leadership
- Staff Personality (warm, sensitive, responsive)
- Teacher/Staff Ratio
- Relaxed and Well Organized
- Safe Indoor and Outdoor Area
- Age-Appropriate Curriculum
- Appropriate Action for Discipline
- Children Clean and Dry
- Plan for Care of Sick of Injured Children

- Safe Place for Children's Medicine
- Code of conduct (discipline and behavior)
- Methods of Learning Playing and Growing
- Comprehensive Family Engaging Activities
- Acts of Communication
- Healthy Nutritious Meals (breakfast, lunch, and snacks)
- Prime Nap Times

Children must have access to opportunities for them to be successful in school and beyond. <u>Parents/Guardians need to use the guidelines of "high-quality" childcare to guide them through the things that will be in place for their children.</u>

Child-Parent Pledge to Learning

At my facility I established A pledge to learn. It is a pledge between the children of ag, that can reasonably comprehend, and their parents. The pledge is that each will want to share the responsibility for student learning. The desire is for our children to develop self-esteem, respect for themselves and others, and a feeling of personal, school, and national pride. It is also imperative that children must behave appropriately, and it is

49

the collective responsibility of the home and school to teach appropriate behavior.

Child: As a child of Kiddie Garden Child Care, I agree:

➢ I will come to childcare prepared to learn. • I will have each day's class activity of homework ready.

➢ I will reach my highest expectations.

➢ I will make my parents aware of all conferences and encourage them to attend.

➢ I will respect my teachers and the school staff.

Parents: I will help my child learn by doing the following:

➢ I will start each day with a calm beginning.

➢ I will make sure my children have a good breakfast, and to get at least eight hours of sleep each night.

➢ I will stress the importance of attendance and that my child needs to be at school every day as long as circumstances permit.

➢ I will keep all lines of communication open with the teachers.

- ➢ I will read to my children every night unless unforeseen situations arise.
- ➢ I will work at home with them and reinforce the skills taught to them at school.
- ➢ I will listen attentively about my child's experiences at school.

CHAPTER 6

Growing Great Minds – The Stages In Childcare

A rthur Fletcher, who was the former head of the United Negro College Fund coined the well-known phrase, *"A mind is a terrible thing to waste."* Everything starts in the mind. The mind is a part of the body that thinks and understands. The mind will become affected by children's attitude's, beliefs, feelings, and thoughts. Children's minds are like "sponges" that absorbs a ton of information. Learning new skills help their minds to grow stronger and help the flow of information.

Learning experiences ensure that children will love to learn and grow. "Knowledge is Power." Knowledge is the factors of the real world rather than a made-up framework. Children's brains are capable of being shaped and changed in their learning engagements. Establishing a deep understanding in children's minds rather than just having them to memorize is very important. This is why instilling layers on layers of knowledge into your curriculum is key. Also, knowledge through consistent core skill development rather than re-inventing the wheel with each lesson is very crucial. The mind of each child must be put into motion along the path of learning. This will in turn prepare them for their journey and will launch them into the future.

I believe that most children are capable of reaching high levels of performance. Even though I've witnessed some children that can be categorized <u>as gifted and talented because they appear to grasp information, instructions and move faster than some others,</u> all children make their way to high performance by flexing their learning muscles.

In the process of "**Growing great minds," we must plant the seeds of curiosity, and children will grow to be life-long learners.** Also keep in mind that approximately 70% of a child's brain is developed by age ONE and approximately 90% of a child's brain is developed by age THREE for future learning demeanor.

When I decided to have my own center, I wanted to create a theme and curriculum that pertained to the growth of the minds of children. So, when I thought about flowers and the process for their growth, I believed that it would be the perfect theme.

The Kiddie Garden Childcare Center will grow great minds in their garden of learners. The commitment of service will be to the following groups and stages of children. Kiddie Garden will provide the highest quality of childcare with the opportunity to have fun and achieve. It will support the emotional, social, and intellectual development of the children in a safe, nurturing family environment. Milestone skills such as talking, smiling, and taking a first steps, will be reached through play, learning, speaking, writing, crawling, and walking.

It will help families endow their children with quality learning experiences, and it will advocate for each child to know that they and their parents and or guardians are loved.

This is the theme and mission statement I presented for my childcare center. So, the concepts which I reference throughout this book will consist of the concept of flowers in a garden.

As was mentioned earlier in this book, children under age 4, that are facing poor health and nutrition, insufficient learning opportunities and more, can have their developmental potential at risk. Tots which are at low achievement levels are at risk of becoming school dropouts. Being raised in a nurturing environment provided by a "High Quality" childcare center presents them with an opportunity to achieve a higher I.Q. and better growth.

Children ages "0-4" are like flowers in a garden. The growing of their minds will be successfully introduced to learning through a systematic concept like the enchantment of flowers in a garden. Their stages will represent the "seed," which will take root. The "sprout" stage will begin to bud, and the "stem" stage will grow, produce, and become a beautiful flower. Children are all different. But just as flowers are all different, together, they make a beautiful garden.

Growing great minds by way of the curriculum can be featured, as well as engaged in one or more of the following ways:

- Grow flowers {like the children in the garden}
- Colors
  - ✓ Numbers
  - ✓ Shapes
  - ✓ Sizes
- Senses {of the flowers provided by the children's brains}
- Smell (nose)
- Eyes (see)
- Fingers (touch)
- Ears (hear)
- Tongue (taste)

When does the story of "little" boys and "little" girls begin? There are at least 5 (five) stages, periods, and/or steps in the process of the development of children. At Kiddie Garden, the stages that the children went through were infants, toddlers, pre-school age and school-age. These three stages were important because they measured growth and maturity. As childcare providers, there are three stages of growth for children from infancy to age 4 which we want to consider. They are as follows:

- SEED STAGE

- SPROUTING STAGE

- BUDDING STAGE

From these stages, the flowers (children) will fully develop into a garden of beautiful inflorescences of learners. Every child, as flowers, is a different kind and color, and all together, they make this world a beautiful garden. As a garden beautifies the earth and gives pleasure to us by a different array of flowers, likewise, children beautify the earth and brings joy and pleasure to us.

STAGES OF GROWTH

Infants: Ages 0-18 months

"Seed Stage"

The Infants ages 0 to 18 months represent the "seed stage." They are just starting to grow. In the "seed stage" an infant is capable of developing learning like the seed of a flower in the garden growing. Just like a seed is planted in soil to receive what it needs to grow, an infant's mind in their seed stage is planted in the soil of information that they may begin to receive what they need to grow. Infant ages 0-18 months are in the "seed stage" and they:

Respond to their name.

Sit without support.

Follow simple instructions.

Toddlers: ages 2 - 3 years
"Sprouting Stage"

The toddlers ages 2 to 3 years represent the "sprouting" stage. They are showing further growth and are producing like sprouts produce and show growth. The "sprouting" of a toddler's mind in the garden of learners is capable of growing like a new bud of a flower. As you can see signs of sprouting when it comes to a flower seed, there is sprouting with children from seed stage to sprout stage.

Toddlers ages 2 - 3 are in the "spouting stage" and so they:

Drink from a cup.

Jump and Climb.

Speak two-word sentences.

Pre-schoolers: ages 3 - 4 years

"Budding Stage"

The pre-school children ages 3 to 4 years represent the "budding" stage. The "budding" of a child in the garden of learners is capable of growth like the stem of a bud grows into a flower. They are now growing to the next level and becoming ready for the next stage of life. Children in the budding stage are considered preschoolers. Pre-schoolers ages 3 - 4 years are in the "budding stage" of a flower and they:

Roll on their back, then roll on their stomach.

Turn pages in a book.

Stand and sit alone.

Children change over the course of childhood as they develop mentally, physically, and socially. All parents/guardians want their children to grow up to be smart, safe, successful, and happy individuals. They have big dreams for their "little" ones the moment of their first steps. However, after pre-school, there are still several more stages children have to go through, and each step has its set of benefits, challenges, and importance.

There are many different ways people explore and describe "little" boys and "little" girls. I will ascribe the following popular nursery rhymes to them. the rhymes may appear in different forms.

What are little boys made of?

Frogs, snails,

and puppy dog tails

That's what little boys are made of.

What are little girls made of?

Sugar and Spice
And all that's nice

That's what little girls are made of.

This rhyme is considered to be "nonsense." But it is an example of a stage of growth. It is a traditional poem or song for children, a fun song to sing and a popular nursery rhyme. When taught to children, it helps them with easy recall and memorization.

The Importance of Structure in Childcare

In order for young minds to bud and grow, it is important for the Childcare center to follow a structured schedule. One is provided below for your consideration.

Day Care Center
Hours of Operation Daily Schedule

7:00 – 9:00 Arrival Time/Free Play

8:00 – 9:00 Breakfast

9:00 – 9:30 Diaper Change/Toileting

9:30 – 9:45 Circle Time/Story Time

9:45 – 10:15 Group Activities

10:45 – 11:15 Outside (Weather Permitting)

11:15 – 11:45 Wash hands for lunch/Lunch Served

11:45 – 12:30 Quiet Time/Diaper Change/Toileting

12:30 – 2:30 Nap Time (The children do not have to sleep, but they do have to lie down or play quietly on their cot so as not to disturb the other children.)

2:30 – 3:00 Diaper Change/Toileting

3:00 – 3:30 Snack

3:30 – 6:00 Free Play/Pick Up Time

***Note:** This a general schedule of your child's daily activities. The schedule may vary due to infant care, special activity days, school schedule, etc.

CHAPTER 7

The Harsh Realities of the Business

Upon opening the doors of my childcare center, I had three children looking forward to a new adventure every day. However, any beginning can be complex and diverse. On the other hand, it can be exciting and rewarding. Each day can be just like life, which is many things, but it is not perfect. Operating the childcare center is a continuous learning process. This chapter is in no way intended to frighten or deter anyone from opening a childcare center. It is designed to inform you of the potential pitfalls and realities that can arise in the business. But for those who possess the will, drive, and endurance, it can be extremely rewarding.

Some very unpleasant realities that involve parents, staff, and children can and will show up.

Being prepared for them in advance is an advantage, in the event that they arise. Taking care of children is a very important job and responsibility. For this reason alone, the staff is an important part of the childcare center. We know that a parent can't be replaced, but the caregivers occupy the place of the children's parents/guardians for the time that they are in the center.

Staff is the biggest and most expensive asset on the childcare budget. Therefore, having good workers on your staff is profitable for your center. Sometimes it makes me upset, but the staff, to put it this way, kind of "carries" the childcare center. That's why I try to develop a good working rapport with the staff when possible. I don't necessarily consider these issues irritating, but it can sometimes be draining. These issues are mentioned below:

Staff unpleasant realities include:

- Being regularly late
- Dressing inappropriately
- Bad attitudes

DR. ELAINE S. MCGHEE

- Disrespectful

- Gossiping

- Absenteeism

- Excessive use of cellphones

- Not team players

- Yelling at the children

- Absence of bonding

- Use of profanity and /or threats

- Disconnected

- Raising voices or yelling

- Smoking excessively

Examples of Staff Issues:

Even though the staff handbook provides the regulations and rules of acceptable procedures and behaviors, many are ignored or disregarded. "Realities" existed but were dealt with. It must be understood that the staff should not be in the place of controlling your business. It is good to inform your workers of what you expect from them. If they are not doing their job, then they run the risk of losing their job. But also remember that your staff, that works well, always appreciates being appreciated.

I had a staff member that lived within walking distance of the childcare center and was late every day, even returning late from breaks.

There were times when appropriate attires were occasionally disregarded. For example, house slippers were worn instead of closed in shoes or sneakers. Stretch pants or leggings were worn instead of jeans or pants, ill-suited tops in place of relevant attire that is practical and comfortable and were not worn by all.

Some smoked during staff breaks and then returned to the classroom, having a horrible stale-smoke odor. It stayed in the air for several hours which may be absorbed through the nose, mouth, or skin of the children. "NO SMOKING" instructions by some were blatantly disregarded.

Some staffers expected to be fed breakfast, lunch, and snacks, like the children were. It was a daily request. But feeding the staff was not a budgeted item.

Preparation and planning lessons in advance affects children's learning, and it takes time to do. Unfortunately, sometimes some staff would put their plans together at the center. On occasions, even ten minutes before class. There were late submissions of lesson plans and misspelled words. It simply meant rushing to plan and not reviewing before submission to the Director. The "icing" on the cake is that lesson plans were usually late or even missing.

There were times when a child was left on the play yard while the rest of the children had returned to class with their teacher. The oversight occurred at least three different times. A required head count was not performed after bringing the children inside.

HELP! There were some staff that were always sending or calling for assistance because a child was out of order. No attempts were made to resolve the situation personally. The discipline policy clearly points out the practice of safety and dealing with disruptive behaviors through praise and positive approaches.

I have had some using their cell phones "24-7" during class and nap time. Received "family emergency" calls on a cellphone that they insisted must be taken. I have encountered employees that exhibited behavior that revealed they were not team players. "Cliques" formed instead.

Turnover of staff was frequently due to insufficient compensation. Some were not willing to pursue additional training to advance their training and to increase their income.

Even though these issues arose with some staff, good staffers make the difference. There are workers that understand their responsibility as a childcare giver and have a love for the job.

Now, let us take a look at some <u>parental issues:</u>

- Cost of Childcare (plus enrolling any additional siblings)

- Lack of available space

- Lack of government investment in early childhood education

- Inconvenient hours for parents (not a babysitter, holiday hours, daily hours)

- Not taking responsibility for child's issues

- Parents bringing 'sick' child to school

Examples of Parent Issues:

Some parents were continuously bringing their children late to school. Failing to understand that emphasis was placed on training for policies and procedures for public or charter school regarding productivity.

There were occasions of late or skipping tuition payments with various excuses. Sometimes taking children out of the childcare center while owing a balance. Therefore, having a contract is necessary if legal actions for payment is required. Remember, you are running a business. Some parents/guardians face circumstances beyond their control, and a few are just careless. It's important to know the difference.

There is the issue of bringing children to school even if they are ill, but claiming they are okay. No doctor's notes because they do not go to one. Home remedies are used.

Pick up time from center is abused. While parents ran errands.

Contact addresses and phone numbers having been changed and the school is not notified of such changes. Communication is made very difficult.

Extra change of clothing in case of emergencies are unavailable. Using clothing which is not theirs is unacceptable.

Some do not attend parent-teacher scheduled meetings or conferences. But children are left for hours in the centers that exceeds the program the parents' contract permits which is unfair and unjust to their child and the staff.

Now let us examine some children's issues.

Children:

Although there are many children brought up "by the book," parents/guardians don't affirm that they will be faultless thereafter. Referring to something I mentioned earlier, some parents/guardians may not know the actuality of unpleasant realities that their child may be affected by. Their interactions with their child may be greater if it is realized. Unpleasant and unexpected realities that parents/guardians face will in one way, shape or form, affect the children. There are times when children act out in negative ways to get others around them worked up. They don't think and want to make others as miserable as they are. Because some children will feel lack of love from their parents/guardians, it can create some issues. When parents/guardians become too busy to interact with their child, it affects them. Also, when they don't take responsibility for their child's negative actions and behaviors, it makes the job a little more challenging. Parents/Guardians need to navigate their journey with their children.

Children's unpleasant realities include:

- Learned negative behavior
- No friends
- High levels of aggression
- Not active in physical activities
- Regularly negative
- Always complaining

Examples of Children Issues:

Many parents side with their children and often blame the teacher. But the children quite often are guilty. Although they are simply exemplifying childlike behavior, it is necessary for the parents to understand that reinforcement of teaching is required. The general situations that arise are these:

- They don't want to listen.

- They don't want to share.

- They don't follow directions.

- They like to bully other children.

- They like to bite other children.

- They like to hit other children.

These were many of the "harsh realities" I had to deal with at my childcare center that I call **"for real, for real"** issues.

Although these issues occurred, at my center, there continued to be an open-door policy for parents.

Unfortunately, there is also the ugly reality of child abuse. This also will cause a child to have behavioral disorders. Therefore, it is to the benefit of your center and the child for courses to be given in recognizing the signs of abuse in the event that it needs to be reported. Abuse can be physical and emotional. Children will get bumps and bruises. But every bump and bruise is not the fault of the child. Don't jump to conclusions. Be alert and observant. Keep the lines of communication open with the parents as much as possible. It will be a help for your center and to the parents/guardians, but most of all for the child. Parents/guardians do have bad days. Assuring them that your care can go a long way.

In spite of the "harsh realities" and "normal realities," childcare centers are necessary and will result in positive development for children and for their success in school.

"Children ages "0-4" are like flowers in a garden for Growing Great Minds."

So, if at first you don't succeed, try, try, and try again.

Every **CHILD is A different**

KIND OF flower,

AND ALL *of them* **TOGETHER,**

MAKE THIS WORLD

A Beautiful

GARDEN.

CHAPTER 8

Overcoming the Challenges of Childcare – Now What???

It is highly likely that "The Harsh Realities of the Business" may have the reader wondering, is it worth it?! When one considers the hassles, it can place doubts in your mind about pursuing a career in childcare. But I must inform you that some of the scenarios are only possibilities. As was mentioned before, the previous chapter was designed to inform you of the potential pitfalls and realities that can arise in the business. In no way did I intend to frighten or deter anyone from opening a childcare center. But for those who possess the will, drive, and endurance, it can be extremely rewarding.

There is a childcare crisis in our country. It is the closing of childcare centers' doors because of the Coronavirus pandemic. For those who are in or started the process for being in the childcare center business, you may have believed that everything was in order. You understand **The Need for High Quality Childcare.** You comprehend that it is **More Than Just Babysitting** and **Understanding the True Purpose of Childcare**. You have prepared for the **Start of Your Childcare Facility and Mission.** You are reasonably astute with the knowledge of **Reaching the Parents of Tots by Understanding Parental Intent,** and **What Parents and Guardians Need to Look for in "High-Quality" Childcare.** You have learned about **The Stages in Childcare,** and **The Harsh Realities of the Business;** But moments arise that cause the strongest people to become fatigued and burdened. When those moments occur, it becomes extremely important to re-focus your energy.

The Coronavirus pandemic is one of those extremely rare events that take place. Because of it, many businesses were affected. It is frustrating enough, with all the other issues that take place; But the effect of the Coronavirus pandemic has caused many to throw in the towel. But if you want your center to rebound from these harsh realities, don't lose your hope. Let me suggest to you what has helped me.

Don't look at the negative, focus on the positive. Don't worry what children will become because, "what they will become, they are in the process of becoming: they will perceive it, they will believe it, and they will achieve it." Dr. Elaine McGhee

We worry about tomorrow, but we forget that children are somebody today. I remember why I started the childcare business. It began with a dream. Even with long hours, hard work, plenty of stress, moments that things went wrong, and some of the children being difficult, for me, the rewards outweighed the challenges. In my experience, the pitfalls and the harsh realities of the **childcare business didn't match the personal satisfaction and emotional rewards that come from the warmth of a child's hug or joy of their laughter, and their success in school.**

I mentioned in the previous chapter, about the challenges of the business; In this chapter I want to do my best to motivate and ignite your passion. Once again, I say that there is the potential and the reality that pitfalls can arise. But for those who possess the will, drive, and endurance, it can be extremely rewarding. I am a prime example that if you maintain the right perspective and focus on the reasons why you went into the childcare business, you can overcome the disappointments and deal with whatever challenges arise.

<u>Focus suggestions for overcoming the challenges in the business.</u>

- Continue to focus on the fact that you are making a difference in a child's life.

- Remember you are helping children to prepare for their future by teaching them the core basics.

- You are helping parents or guardians shape the minds of their children

- You are assisting in teaching children to respect authority

- You are assisting in teaching children social skills and how to play and work with others.

- As a seed is planted in the soil and nurtured, you are planting children in the soil of knowledge and information that will stay with them for a lifetime.

- What children learn from you and with you, can make a difference in their educational performance in their future.

- You are helping to build self-awareness and self-esteem in children.

- You will be involved, not only in helping children socially, but physically, mentally, and academically.

Therefore, I encourage anyone that is in the business, and will be in the business of childcare, to stay motivated, enthusiastic, driven, empowered and uplifted. Why? Because childcare is still needed and always will be. Learning doesn't stop, and YOU will be making a difference! It is essential to continue to develop the skill that children will need for success in school as well as for their lives outside of school. By the age of 4 years old, stages of developmental growth or milestones do not stand still.

Something additional to be considered is the procurement of an appropriate childcare license to include school-aged children, ages five to 12 years old. It can be an integral part of the incorporation of an afterschool program. Children continuously grow and new skills are added as they grow.

An afterschool program can have a tremendous impact on children's academics, self-esteem, and over-all happiness. These afterschool programs are growing in number. It will bring peace of mind for parents knowing that their children are in a healthy, safe, environment. Their school assignments will be completed, as well as an opportunity to participate in activities and play. Healthy, appropriate snacks will also be provided. The afterschool program within the childcare centers can be used to service the afterschool students, between the possible closing of their home and school at 3:00 p.m. and 6:00 p.m., who would then be picked up by their parents.

Both childcare and afterschool childcare centers are fun, busy, active, healthy, secure, and safe. It is essential to continue to develop the skills that the children will need to meet the challenges of life, learning, and love for the future.

In the very familiar poem, *"Children Learn What They Live,"* by Dr. Dorothy Law Nolte, she highlights some of the lessons from life that are important to be mentioned and practiced which would assist in meeting the challenges at home and at school.

"If children live with encouragement, they learn confidence."

"If children live with kindness and consideration, they learn respect."

"If children live with praise, they learn appreciation."

"If children live with acceptance, they learn love."

I started an afterschool program at my center for that very reason. It was **"The Kiddie Garden Childcare/Afterschool Childcare Center 2."**

The childcare centers may appear to be all play, but they are key to reinforcing the importance of having a good educational foundation. This foundation of learning will carry over into school years and will include the following:

- School Readiness
- Shaping Children's Brain
- Homelike Environment
- Flexible Hours
- Necessity for Working Parents
- Making Friends
- Learning to Socialize
- Reduced Stress for Parents
- Learning the Basics
- Parents Continue to have Two Incomes
- Long Lasting Benefits
- Children's Safety, Health, and Happiness
- Social and Learning Skills
- Structure
- Independence

Every child should be given the positive experiences and nurturing which they need and deserve. Investing in tomorrow's future is critical.

"Learn from the start. A great start goes a long way!"

Day Care

Following is a Typical School Calendar:

Sept. 7   Holiday: Labor Day
       8   School Begins
Oct. 12   Holiday: Indigenous People's Day
            observance)
Nov. 5-6   NJEA Convention
       9   Holiday: Veteran's day (observance)
      10   Holiday: Puerto Rico Heritage's Day
            (observance)
      15   Early Dismissal (1:00 p.m.)
   26-27   Holiday: Thanksgiving
Dec.   3   Parent/Teacher Conferences (1:00
            p.m. dismissal)
      23   Early Dismissal (1:00 p.m.)
      24   Holiday: Christmas Eve
      25   Holiday: Christmas Day
   28-30   Winter Recess
      31   Holiday: New Year's Eve
Jan.   1   Holiday: New Year's Day
      18   Holiday: Martin Luther King's
            Birthday (observance)
Feb. 12   Holiday: Lincoln's Birthday
            (observance)
      15   Holiday: President's Day
      18   Parent/Teacher Conferences (1:00
            p.m. dismissal)
April 2   Holiday: Good Friday
     5-9   Spring Recess

May   12   Holiday: Eid-al-Fitr
   31   Holiday: Memorial Day
June 28   Last day of School

Note: The Day Care Center calendar shown is for the purpose of showing the events of the school year. The dates will most certainly change, but the basic format will relatively remain the same. Although some businesses are closed on certain holidays, many centers remain open.

*(observance is optional for the days for center closures).

CHAPTER 9

The "Original "Three Children" Who Played, Learned and Grew Together

The three children that entered the childcare center were seven months old, and they remained through Pre-K. They are now 6 years old and started second grade in September 2021.

Preschool benefits were real and are continuing to be in their regular school years and will be on-going beyond! **All they really needed to know, they learned in Kiddie Garden Childcare Center.**

They learned through play, exploration, and hands-on observation. Their minds were like sponges soaking up everything in their beginning stages at the childcare center. They were able to take in so much which did nothing but help. Also, they were provided with a foundation for learning in a structured setting.

The children were excited, parents were nervous, teachers were competent, and it was our responsibility at the center, and all involved to lead the children on the pathway to a successful partnership toward achieving the following:

- Identify letters in the alphabet

- Write their names (print)

- Trace letters in the alphabet and numbers

- Identify shapes and size difference

- Count to 100

- Identify animals and their sounds

- Know community workers

The childcare center's staff and administrators took them by their hands, opened their minds, and touched their hearts. They are currently socially, physically, mentally, and academically successful.

CONCLUSION

I wrote hard and clean about what hurts. I was guided to point out the truth about childcare centers for your child, their services, and how to protect your investment by becoming aware of the "real, real" realities in owning and/or directing one. Both our parents, and our children deserve nothing but the best! The basis for a childcare center is trust through a warm, supportive, and dependable contact with each child as well as established strong support for family bonding and meeting the unique needs of the proposed age groups. The life cycle of a seed's journey to a plant illustrates a child's journey to academic success.

"Children don't care how much you know until they know how much you care!" Teddy Roosevelt.

Let us remember this quote by former President Barak Obama.

"Change will not come if we wait for some other person, or if we wait for some other time. We are the ones we've been waiting for. We are the change that we seek."

Information About Grants and Financing

Early Childhood Education Advocates, Inc.

Here is How $39 Billion will Be Spent on Child Care.

$39 billion in Child Care. Nearly $15 billion in Child Care and Development Block Grant (CCDBG)

- States are authorized to provide childcare assistance to healthcare sector employees, emergency responders, sanitation workers, and other workers deemed essential regardless of the
- Income eligibility requirements under the Child Care and Development Block Grant Act.
- Nearly $24 billion for newly created childcare stabilization grants.
  - Each lead agency will receive a childcare stabilization grant.
- Lead agencies will reserve not more the 10% of grant funds to administer, promote, and/or assist childcare providers in applying for subgrants.

- Lead agency will use remaining funds to make subgrants to qualified childcare providers regardless of a provider's previous receipt of Federal assistance.
- Qualified – means an eligible childcare provider – that on the date of application, submission was either: open/available to provide childcare services or closed due to public health/financial hardship/other COVID – 19 related reasons.
- Eligible means:
  - Those defined under section 658P of the Child Care and Development Block Grant Act of 1990
  - Or a childcare provider licensed, regulated, and registered in the state on the date of enactment and meets applicable state and local health and safety requirements.
- Grant amount based on operating expenses
  - Restriction: Cannot reduce compensation, including benefits, that an employee was receiving as of date of submissions.
  - Requirement: Provider also will provide relief from copayments/tuition payments for families enrolled in their program to the extent possible

- Funds need to be used for at least one of the following:
  • Personnel costs
  - Rent
  - PPE
  - Purchasing equipment/supplies to respond to COVID – 19
  - Goods/services necessary for the services provided
  - Mental health supports for children/employees
- Funds can be used to reimburse a provider for expenditures made prior to the enactment of this Act for the cost of a good/service that is permitted under this Act to respond to COVID – 19 public health emergencies. In other news, the ECEA is supporting an assembly bill appropriating $10 million in federal funds to be used by the state Economic Development Authority to support childcare centers in need in New Jersey. The bill (S. 3520) is now before the Senate Budget Committee.

Based on information on March 22, 2021 from Jaffe Communications

ABOUT THE AUTHOR

Dr. Elaine S. McGhee has been in the education field for quite some time. She received her high school diploma from South Side High School (currently Shabazz High School) in Newark NJ.; B.S. Commerce Degree from Rider University in Trenton, NJ.; M.A. Degree from Jersey City State College, (currently New Jersey City University) in Jersey City NJ.; Student Personnel Services Certificate from Montclair State (currently Montclair University) in Montclair, NJ; Doctor of Education, ED. D. from Nova Southeastern University in Fort Lauderdale, Florida. Dr. McGhee has more teaching experiences and guidance counseling that is not currently included in this bio. A retired educator, Dr. McGhee served as an Elementary and a Secondary School Teacher, Guidance Counselor, and Administrator in Essex, Hudson, and Union Counties. She also served as the supervisor of Pulpit Personnel Service, Essex County College Professor, Seton Hall University Upward Bound Associate Director, Project GRAD Newark College Scholarship Manager, and Director of her own family Daycare Center, (closed due to Covid-19).

She is the proud parent of two adult children and grandmother of one grandchild. She states that the blessing of her life are her two awesome children, Darren and Elissa and a phenomenal granddaughter, Shaniah.

ORDER INFORMATION

You can order additional copies of this book by emailing the author directly using the email address below.

Dr. Elaine S. McGhee

Email Address: eeartdr@aol.com

Books are available at Amazon.com, BN.com Kindle and Your Local Bookstores (By Request)

Please leave a review for this book on Amazon and let other readers know how much you enjoyed reading it.

Thank you!

www.ingramcontent.com/pod-product-compliance
Lightning Source LLC
Chambersburg PA
CBHW060552100426
42742CB00013B/2535

*9 7 8 1 7 3 7 4 8 4 0 8 0 *